CW00420112

Letters

to

Rosie

By

Love Charmer

CONTENTS

Letters To Rosie

INTRODUCTION

This book is an anthology of poems dedicated to my wife. These poems were written to express my love to her at various points in our lives. They depict my views on our divine union, courtship, holy matrimony and beyond. I zoom in on our focal point of love!

ABOUT THE AUTHOR

Love Charmer is a budding poet. As a shy kid, writing was a way to express his voice. Presently he uses his writing in different literary art forms to be heard across the globe. He was born in the sunny archipelago of The Bahamas.

CHAPTER ONE

Divine intervention

On this auspicious occasion,
An angel descended from heaven.
I wasn't prepared for the invasion,
Far less for a wedding.
Small greetings began this equation.
Our destiny combined so perfectly like the
number seven.
However, our differences needed much
more persuasion.

She was out of my league to the world,
But my heart kept pressing.
My thoughts meshed to reflect a
beautiful Trinidadian.
We were used to existing singular,
Like two ones in the number eleven.
Her smile grew on me like a fortune cookie
to a wise Asian.

Through it all I had to play it cool.
I often used other guests as a diversion.
In the eyes of others, on this day we
starred at the pool.

In our eyes, our show was kept private
behind a curtain.
I could feel my heart drool.
The butterflies fled for freedom, leaving
my stomach hurting.
I was never sure of any exams at school,
But on this day, I met my wife, I was
certain!

From the day my mom passed, my heart
has been in detention.
I would have never approached love
unless it was done forcefully.
This encounter made my hairs stand at
attention.
I was still treading very cautiously.

Barely flirting, instead I soaked her in
graciously.
As a friend, I managed to ask her out
courageously.
Magically, she accepted.
I was overjoyed at not being rejected.

In many more years to come, this date
will be reflected.
To have this angel as my wife was my
only intention.
Did I forget to mention,
This union, for me, was definitely a divine
intervention!

Dreamy beginning

When I think of you,
You make my emotions collide.
This feeling is out of this world!
God sent this angel to be by my side.
That's why, I promise to love you with pride.
We find beauty in ordinary things.
So please do not hide.
Or dream of loosing this ability.
There's no need to trap your feelings deep inside.

Your love jingles my heart every time your soul receives me.
It's coming straight from my heart,
I hope you believe me.
Not even death could make us part.
As long as you don't deceive me.
I don't want you to ever think about leaving me.

A gambler will not only lose what he has,
But also what he doesn't have.
For you, I have weak knees.
Yet I'm standing straight while enjoying
this cool love breeze.
I'm starting this new year hoping you
would always be mine.
Not only during Christmas times or
Valentines!

My English love

When I think of England,
I see London Bridge falling down,
And you're standing tall.
When I think of England,
The queen has lost her crown!
Her majesty's reign begins to fall.

When I think of England,
I don't see the Thames River,
Just your long flowing hair!
When you're next to Big Ben you make my
heart shiver,
To see you look so lovely and fair!
Your love makes me quiver like I'm naked
at winter.

When I think of England,
I see you through the London Eye.
Your love can't hide from me!
But thinking of England has made me cry.
Expressing this feeling means the world
to me.

Especially when I remember how our love used to be!

Like, when we took the underground to switch to the over ground,
Trying to make a grand escape from Finsbury Park.
I'm reflecting on England without making a sound.
I'm praying that this poem reaches your heart.
I never plan to convert you like a dollar to a pound.
Like your guardian angel, I will shed light when your skies are dark!

Let's be friends

Let's be friends,
Hmm.....
I guess we've passed the end.
Although you say you will be there all the
way,
I feel like we've gone astray.
It's like we have taken a wrong turn,
while we allow our hearts to burn.
Friends or family may not agree.
In my reality, it doesn't matter to me!
I'm in it for you.
Will you love me for who I am, or will it be
for who you want me to be?

I may not have gold or materialistic
glitter.
All I have is a loving soul.
There is no more space for litter.
Be careful with alterations,
If you pull the wrong thread everything
could fall apart.

Sleepless nights;
Long days dreaming;
Some lovely fights,
Leaving our hearts steaming.
This episode shines different lights.
You gave my life a new meaning!

If I die today,
It would be in silence.
No more regrets and nothing more to say.
No more fighting, bringing an end to the
imaginary violence.
Some thoughts are stuck on replay.
This experience has surely given me
guidance!

Let's be friends,
Hmm.....
I don't know how to demote my feelings
or let them go.
Friendly love may be harmless but my love,
My true feelings will always show.

Imagine being idle while the one you love
walks away.
In reverence I pray,
And read through my bible.
Analysing, while trying to compromise.
Realising you won't have my title.
Or worse yet, what will we do when it's
time to move on?
You live happily ever after, while I sing a
sad song?
I may be wrong,
But the future is my rival.
I won't have the courage to face it,
Knowing that your love is gone!
I need you by my side to fight this
friendly battle.

Love desires

My love is coming straight from my heart
and soul.
You are the one becoming my treasure of
gold.
From love we aren't running, your heart
I'll cherish and hold.
People are cunning but our love will grow
old.
Your natural glow is beyond stunning!
With you I'm aiming to take a stroll.
We will have our smiles beaming even
when it's cold.
I'm very sorry for being bold,
But my love story you stole.
With our heads steaming, our love can be
moulded into a roll.
It doesn't matter how they're scheming,
your love will never be sold.
I know I'm not dreaming because I see
the mixture in a bowl.
We are on top of love's bridge and
underneath lives the troll.

There is a mystery to everything that has been told.

When we are together it's like I've scored a winning goal.

When you are away, it feels like I've been hit by a spinning pole.

We need to take hatred and bury it in a never ending hole.

Then take our love pieces and make them whole.

I'll be a comforter to you like a sole.

I'll be soft and sweet like a fairytale retold.

You're mine forever!

You're the one I'll behold.

Please love me back because I feel like I'm going out of control.

Every year I want to take you to the super bowl.

There you would see the important question on the ticket console.

Whatever your answer, I promise to understand and not scold.

Belief in love

For you, I'm ready to go to war.
I'm sure you know what I have in store.
If not, come into my heart and take a tour.
This precious love will have you begging for more.
I believe in our love!

I want to lift you to the seventh floor.
Once you've witnessed my love, you'll be sure.
Sure that this relationship is real and pure.
I want our love to be even, like the number four.
I believe in our love!

I can't wait to land this ship ashore.
I want us to be face to face,
Not hiding behind the brokenness of our history's door.
We won't be checking for the clothes we wore,

Or any past memories we tore.
When we are sick, we will need each
other's love to be the cure.
I'm dreaming about how this love will
over pour.
I believe in our love!

You make me believe in love.
Furthermore, I believe in me and you.
I believe in miracles.
There's beauty in the little things we do.
My belief trumps magical rituals.
My belief in love and destiny helps keep my
heart pure and true!
A strong belief can join any two individuals!

Confession of love

This obsession is my confession.
I've found love through your eyes!
You're my final decision made with
precision.
I choose you to be my prize!
My love has no exaggeration or
refrigeration.
There shall be no cries.

Until I have your attention to feel
redemption,
I'll remove all of the lies!
There doesn't have to be any degradation
for a relation.
That's a word from the wise!
You will be a blessing or a lesson.
But behind the heartache remains the
tries!

Please say yes to the collection of my affection.
I'll make it the right size!
My heart's love is because of erosion but it's afraid of decomposition.
That phase attracts too many flies!

Take my love into consideration.
I'm softer than marshmallow pies!
There's no type of collision to cause division.
From the ashes we shall rise and change our lives!

True love

It's been a while since I've seen your
face.
My heart begins to listen as your lips
begin to speak.
The story your eyes tell when they
glisten, makes my muscles weak.

The taste of your love showed me that
you're the one I need.
You sold me words that you didn't mean.
But you gave me the privilege to see how
much you've changed.
It was all in the right way.
That's why I love you.

I believe your love for me is true.
I'll always love you; I'll keep on loving you!
I don't know why.
I'm yours, you can tell me what to do.

The search is over!

Looking at your face,
I know I've found love at last!
To your heart I race,
Not trying to move too fast.
You took my soul to a place,
Where love has no contrast.

Looking deep into your eyes,
I realise I've found love for sure!
I see you as my prize,
You lifted my spirits off the floor.
Physically you're the right size,
And for my love issues, you're the heaven
sent cure.
I hope you noticed the tries,
To keep my love for you pure.

I'm finally feeling you in my arms and soul,
Never wanting to let you go!
For the love of my life, my goal is to let
this budding love grow.
Teach me how to keep my love under
control.

Teach me all I need to know,
We shall become in sync like the current
moving with the river's flow.
We'll be so much as one, that our hearts
will be warm amidst the deepest snow!

A love letter

Dear my love,
To your soul my heart reaches,
Trying to hold onto something so real!
It's more than just your sweetness,
Or the physical attraction I feel.
I stare through the meekness,
As my body tries to deal,
With this unusual weakness.
I want us to be like sand to the beaches;
Like cream mixed with peaches;
Like a professor who always teaches;
Yet, my heart remains speechless.
I can't find the voice to preach this,
But I feel the deepness,
As my scars begin to heal.

Listen with your heart, as my soul begins
to speak.
It's your never ending love that makes
my knees weak!
You're my comforter while I sleep!
The lights to my street!

We're not featured on the billboard chart,
even though that would be neat.
For me, falling in love with you is my
biggest feat!
Only God can understand this treat that
I eat!
You're definitely a treasure to keep!

When I look upon the stars, it's dim lights
I see up there!
Because in my eyes, the stars can't
outshine you my dear!
My heart cries, whenever I sense that
you're near.
The sun hides, away from your beauty!
I'm in dreamland searching for your
smoochie.
The moon smiles down at your glowing
physique.
And I love that you're very unique!

With each breath you take, you've left me amazed!
You're that healthy shake that sets my heart ablaze!
This thunderous earthquake has a lasting effect that stays!
So don't blame me if I do nothing else but gaze!
I hope to never wake up out of this phase.
You're my velvet cake that's perfectly glazed!
I'm in awe at your eternal bliss!
I feel blessed to possess a love like this.
I'm on one knee waiting to taste your heavenly kiss!

Letters To Rosie

CHAPTER TWO

Wedding bliss

From the first day we met, I promised to tie the knot.
A few years later, we used the exact spot for our plot.
The beach setting was beautiful and the sun was blazing hot.
I must say this remains on top, especially given the rocky road we trot.
For you my dear, my love will never stop.

On the wedding day, the sun stood still as the events rolled pass.
Inside I was nervous, while outside my look was chilled.
Twenty four hours never moved so fast.
Many emotions were spilled.
Within this intimate gathering there was love from our supporting cast.

It was a great accomplishment to climb to the top of this hill.
She's lawfully mine now, for permission I don't have to ask.

There no longer has to be that guilty
feeling, like borrowing some meat from
the grill.
In the beauty of our moment we were
gearing up for future tasks.

One was living together and sharing our
bills.
For now, in the glory my soul continues to
bask.
Surely I look forward to enjoying many
more thrills.
Like the sand ceremony that was
beautifully displayed in a flask.

All went well until I started to feel ill.
My eyes were twitching like a potato
waiting to be hashed.
Even though that morning they were
doused in eye drops with the most
convincing skill.
As the sun had set, the dream cloud
began to latch.

Throughout the Breezes resort we
glowed like new coins in a till.
Better yet, we looked crisp and
scrumptious like a fresh cookie batch.

To love her is easier than growing gills.
To cap it all off, we enjoyed the private
cabanas with roofs that were thatched.
We will grow with each other until our
souls become attached.

The challenge is always staying in love.
Especially as we face our differences and
the temptations of this world.
In the centre we keep God from above.
From day one to now, I'm truly in love
with my girl!
My wedding bliss descended upon me like a
dove.
It was the most special and exotic
Bahamian pearl.

My vows to you

This obsession is my confession. I found love through your eyes. You're my final decision made with precision. I choose you to be my prize!

A smile from you is like a single raindrop in the middle of a desert. It's very refreshing and always has me thirsting for more! Your smile means everything to me.

I vow to make you smile even through the hardest day. This is one for the archives! One that God neither his angels will forget. And even if they do, our hearts will never forget. No one could fathom the depth of our love. It flows deeper than the ocean.

I would not trade this moment right here, right now, to be anywhere else in this world or in any other world, my love! Each day you say you love me, just know that I love you more!

My Angel Forever!

There's nobody in the world but you and I!
Our love blossoms vividly as each day
passes by.
My soul is lucky to be infatuated with you.
Furthermore, you strengthen our crew.
You grant me the most luxurious view.
With each sight, you make my love feel
brand new.
You're beautiful without make up too.
You're my Angel Forever!

When I need motivation,
Just a glance of you makes my heart
believe.
Now you can call me a believer.
To love you, is all I want to achieve.
You are what makes me a great achiever.
On any stressful day, a glimpse of you is
my greatest stress reliever.
I thank God for giving me more than a
cheerleader,
You're my Angel Forever!

Girl you are my angel,
The love of my life!
You're the secret ingredient to my recipe.
I'm honoured to have you as my wife!
Our hearts have coincided with destiny.
My darling angel,
You mean the world to me.
You're my Angel Forever!

I'm going to love you,
I pray I don't ever lose you.
I want to hold you,
And remind you daily why I love you.
I will never take you for granted.
Nor forget the memories we've planted.
The fruit of our love will never go rancid.
With an angel like you, our love can
withstand it!
You're my Angel Forever!

Happy First Christmas.....as my wife!

To have you by my side is a blessing always,
Whether we're stuck by a roadside or decking the hallways.
We've been jolly and had a land marking November.
Like a silver and gold trolley, it's definitely a year to remember!

I will love you with much pride.
You always add an extra pep to my stride,
Making my temperature rise higher than the sunrays.

Some memories are too perfect to forget, like our first married Christmas!
I hope it brings you much happiness as loving you has brought me.
My "Trini Goddess", please hold me,
And live happily forever!
Merry Christmas!

Happy First Valentine's Day.....as my wife!

This day is not new to us.
It's new to the world.
The universe watches with popping eyes
of lust,
Marvelling at how our hearts curl.

My love, like blood flows to a liver,
You give me that energetic blast.
It doesn't matter how much we differ,
using a table of contrast.
Our love surfaces deeper than the
Mississippi River, with one big splash!
Although our souls quiver, reaching away
from our spirit's grasp.

It's true, in God we trust!
He is a major part of our swirl.
I can't fathom how he didn't fuss,
The day he made you my girl!

I had a barren field of love with nothing
to deliver.
I prayed and now I'm fruitful at last!
Now our armour shines brighter than
silver,
while our hearts shimmy away from the
past.

We are glorious amongst any fine dust.
We're truly a diamond in this rough world.
We have travelled a long way of disgust,
Allowing destiny to unfold.

Now our love is under a filter.
Our hearts are being cleansed from trash.
All because of our dynamic builder,
Who doesn't need to be paid in cash!

He makes our love tougher than an
elephant's tusk.
And he eliminates visits to the doctor.
Like a double decked bus,
we have massive roads to conquer!

Valentine's love

Oh my Pinto, my Nina, my Santa Maria,
You are my greatest discovery.
I don't think my heart could have made a
better recovery.
You're truly my golden treasure!

You brighten the stars when the nights
are dim.
You increase my moonlight when the
evening is slim.
I promise to cherish you forever!

Especially at night when you sleep ever so
peacefully,
You have that look of pure beauty that
makes my heartbeat race increasingly.
To give away those moments, I'll say
never!

Our love is as smooth as a baby's skin.
And it's sharper than a beard that has
just been trimmed.
We're truly meant to be together!

I thank you Lord for 7.11.2015.
That's the day my angel descended from
heaven and out of my dream.
With God, we can withstand any stormy
weather!

Glory and praises be unto Him.
For He controlled our hearts,
He cleansed us of our sins,
He allowed us to live the love we were
destined.
You're truly my Angel Forever!

You came true and free of any mockery.
With a woman like you by my side, there is
nothing stopping me.
On this day, there is nothing better.
I couldn't have gotten anything better!

Happy Valentine's Day!

Happy First Birthday..... as my wife!

Your birthday is another chance for me to tell you how special you are.
And how much you will always mean to me.
You are my first and only bright star.
I'm always grateful our hearts agree.

Each year, you have new hopes, dreams and so many wonderful memories.
It's just your first married birthday and as far as forever seems, we will get there and make it part of our summaries.

We will march into the future together.
All I need is me and you.
I know that each day of each new year would be a perfect one, as long as I have you.

Happy Birthday!

Our First Anniversary

Despite feeling stressed at times,
I'm grateful to be blessed at all times.
It's a joy to know that you're mine.
Our souls were caressed beyond the pines.
Our hearts let out lots of distressed
chimes.

We've been lost and our eyes have been
dried.
We're not willing to pay the pricey cost, so
with love we've tried and tried.
This vigorous battle was rightly fought.
Our hearts have cried and learnt the
lessons taught.
They will heal all the feelings caught.

It's amazing how small greetings began
this equation.
And one little question led to such a big
adventure, filled with everything we
dreamt of and more!

And even though "I do" seems like just yesterday, it will always be the happiest day of my life!

Happy Anniversary
One year down, forever to go!

Letters To Rosie

CHAPTER THREE

Rosie

Rosie, Rosie, how I miss your hugs!
That warmth is always cosy and gets me
hooked worse than drugs.
For your love I will be nosy, sniffing for it
even under rugs.

Right now we are swimming in a deep
situation.
Our future hinges on the immigration
federation.
In the meantime we face this vile
monster of separation.
At times we stare at our pictures out of
desperation,
Reminiscing on the times we shared and
praying for an intervention.
Hopefully all the pain and distress is taken
into consideration following this
application,
Especially the loving hearts torn in this
situation.

Lonely nights, praying days, hopeful
hearts and faithful souls!
I'm missing my wife like the precious air
to my lungs.
I'm missing making her laugh and running
my fingers through her hair.
She is my staff, the only one I lean on in
times of fear.

But all will be well!
This trial will not be in vain.
In our hearts is where God dwells,
To keep us from going insane.
He witnessed our hearts swell,
While enduring this great amount of pain.
And Willy Boy could tell,
Things won't be the same!

Symbol of love

I may not be a photographer but every
day I can only picture us together.
I know if I'm only fighting for treasure,
this battle may last forever.
I may not be a mechanic but when I'm
with you, your love fixes my lever.
Your smile brightens my day, it prepares
my mind to face whatever.
I may not be a scholar but your presence
makes me clever.
You unlock my brilliance like wine aging in a
cellar.

A love like this is made for the public.
My dear, whenever your heart feels tired
I will massage it.
Similarly, as meat marinates in seasoning
laced with garlic,
Your beauty is vibrant like scarlet.
I'm not a chocolatier but I can convert
you to a chocoholic.
The love we share will forever be symbolic.

It represents all of the recovering
alcoholics.
As bubbly as it sounds my dear, our love is
far from being diabolic.

I'm not a politician but I debate for your
love.
I believe a love like this is worth arguing
for.
Whenever the world turns to mindless
birds, you remain graceful like a dove.
With each step you take, your light glows
some more.
You are like the sun, your heat burns
brightly from above.
Your flames energise my core.
I don't play baseball but daily I'm
catching feelings for you like when a ball
falls into a glove.
And like a shopkeeper, memories of you are
all I store.

I'm not a pest but only you I would bother.
At times I know this love makes you feel a bit smothered.
There's no way of separating a sister and brother.
I may not be a priest but I ensure our union is covered.
We are protected like a baby shielded by its mother.
While the universe is walking, our love is being hovered.
This love is out of this world!
It definitely can't be compared to any other.
I still can't believe it's not buttered.
Your flavour satisfies my heart like a poem to a lover.
Meanwhile, my spirit will feed on your love and I pray that not a sound will be uttered!

A Christmas apart

In thought, we are never far apart,
From the people we hold closely in our
heart.
Because of your love, this hill I'm not
afraid to climb.

We will still have the countless calls at
night.
Though the distance and busy schedules
keep us from talking as often as we would
like,
It doesn't keep me from thinking about
you, caring for you or wishing you a very
Merry Christmas!

It's a heartbreaking one,
But I'm grateful for the trials.
It will only make us stronger as we climb.
I believe God will restore our union
because it's vital!

Christmas' apart will soon be a thing of
the past.
Something we would reflect on for
motivation.
This distance will not be in vain.
In fact, it will support us like a cast.
Because of our separation, we will be
drawn together with much less pain!

Beautiful love

Remembering your love keeps my heart in check.
This awesome feeling helps me find serenity.
I thank the father above,
He has all of my respect!
To his gates of love, I'll be leaning seeking the holy trinity.
You remind me of a dove with a graceful neck.
And like a beautiful key ring, you bang my soul past infinity.
You protect my spirits like a glove and capture my harmony in your net.
Our love pours past the ceiling.
Thanks to this new found energy that will keep us going for all eternity.
Into the future our hearts we shove.
The world isn't ready yet!
They have the audacity to keep disbelieving,
That our hearts reside in their own city!

Spousal bliss

This is an awesome pleasure,
One that will last now and forever.
To enjoy a beautiful wife like this, in a
heartless life like this!

I'm just here wishing we could be
together,
So we could enjoy this turbulent weather.
Our "brollys" are tired of all the turns and
twists.
And our bodies crave for heat to warm
our fists.
It's like we don't own our treasure.

Our minds have tried to be clever.
Without a magic wand, we perform tricks.
We've had some glory moments, enjoyed
with some luxurious crisps.
It was well seasoned with salt and black
pepper.

We take in the lessons and pray for
better.

I'm grateful regardless, especially for all
your flicks.
You've softened the trials and removed
our cemented bricks.

You're my sweet caramel, my buttery
popcorn and my honey dew.
Each day my soul is filled of you.
You're sweeter than a bar of Twix.
Just the thought of your magnificent love
gives my being an extra kick!

You're more than dreamy, especially your
luscious lips.
You are like a moon ride, taking my soul on
countless trips!
Your love is like water, it has essential
drips.
You fill my heart and hold my love with a
tight grip.
I'm grateful to have a beautiful wife like
this, in a dreadful life like this!

Letters To Rosie

CHAPTER

FOUR

Love kept us

It's been a heartfelt blessing to reach
such a prestigious milestone.
And now my soul feels more at home.
You can consider me "Trini to D bone".

This amazing love is too much!
Anything is enhanced by your touch.
Especially, the "Wi-Fi King" and his smart
phone.
Anytime I reminisce, it becomes a happier
tone.
I vow that we will never be alone.
Divine intervention will always be near
protecting our unique gemstone.
God is our buoyant force.
No matter how strong the winds or how
gigantic the waves are, our love will never
sink because we are anchored to him.

I'm grateful to stay afloat with you,
even if the water is icier than morning
dew.
Your amazing love shall keep me warm.
No speed bump can tear us apart.
It doesn't matter the size or form.
With a love like this, we will conquer any
storm!

Destiny

Rosie,
You are my destiny!
Yeah, you've got the best of me!
Thinking of your kisses takes my soul past ecstasy!
You know that I love you.
So I'll give you nothing less, you see!

Rosie,
I'm on my knees thinking of what you mean to me.
My thoughts go so deep while I'm sipping some Hennessey.
Being in love with you is all I want to see!
You took my soul, my heart and all I could ever be.
Now we're growing old like a sapodilla tree!

We were destined to love.
I believe our hearts were connected since our creation by the one who resides above.
Even when we wanted to go our separate ways, destiny didn't permit.
Countless were the days, when we both felt to quit!

We weren't forced but clearly we were meant for each other.
Our connection is deeper than a sister's to a brother.
I thank God I was destined to be your lover and protector.
Presently, our destiny of love remains our strongest cover!

Embracing destiny

Our love is like mature cheddar, well grated.
Our souls glisten like gold, just like your MK pieces that are gold plated.
Like wild thoughts, our love can't be contemplated.
For you, my soul has many speeches.
Yet it can't be debated.
Like sand to the beaches, our hearts are over populated.
But those residents can't be decapitated, because they ensure our love is well insulated.
No one can ever say that our love is over rated, especially when that view is speculated.

This love can't be calculated.
Neither can it be manipulated.
To be with you my dear, could never be traded.

It doesn't matter how many times the lights have faded.
Each night I'm thanking God for the best angel ever created.
My love, just know I love you more, even when it's not stated.
Your love is too precious and rare to be treated anything less than sacred.
Each day I aim to ensure that my vows are reinstated.

Your love is sweet, meek and like anything heaven related.
Just like an airplane, your love keeps me well "aviated".
I enjoy every second that my Angel Forever is activated.
I hope your wings remain well inflated.
My love, like a ray of light on my darkest night, you mean the world to me.
I could lose my sight or die of fright yet, next to you is where I long to be.
I will always try to make things right when evil gives our love a fight.
Let's embrace our destiny.

Our second Anniversary

It's our second anniversary now and yes,
our love is stronger than day one!
There is no heat hotter than this under
the sun.
I pray that God continues to guide this
one, so our love may not be done.
It's hard to find its origin.
Only God knows where it's from.
Two plus two equals me and you, yet the
world still acts a bit dumb.
Like this love being doubled is too much
fun and it leaves their eyes numb.

It feels like it was just yesterday when I
was serving you drinks at the Breezes
pool bar.
Just yesterday, I didn't know what to
say as we took pictures in front of
Bahamar.
Just yesterday, I honeymooned in the UK,
my first time travelling so far.
This journey was way beyond my radar.

Just yesterday, you would pay to visit a
spa.
And to this day, your love fills my cookie
jar.

The first anniversary has passed.
It was phenomenal!
It now belongs to history.
It's recorded in my journal,
And etched perfectly in my memory.
It keeps me dressed formal,
And quickly changes my summary.
Your love reveals the secret recipe made
by the Colonel.
No longer is it a mystery.

We grow together.
We're like a baby, developing ever so
delicately.
I plan to enjoy your love feverishly,
Even if I'm laid to rest in my tomb.
Our love has grown deliciously,
Sweeter than a honeycomb.
You're truly my Angel Forever!

Anniversary reflections

It seems like yesterday when we both
said I do,
And I began that wonderful journey of
sharing my life with you!
Those reflections will never be blue.
Whenever we stumble on a problem, we
could look back to find a clue.

It only seems like yesterday when we
walked down the aisle,
And my heart was filled with everlasting
love at the sight of your beautiful smile.
That warmth flows through my memories
all the while.
I'll forever enjoy this reflective style.

It only seems like yesterday but one sure
thing is true.
I'm more in love with you than when we
first said I do.

Happy Anniversary
Two years down, forever to go!

Engraved love

As years flew by, your love grew on me.
So, I scratched it somewhere sacred,
somewhere only you can be.
This love has been etched perfectly.
You're my love and one true family.
As I engrave your love to my heart, my
soul remains exposed.
Your love shall never depart even if the
sex window is closed.
This tattoo shall be marked very high, on
a level only you and I can reach.
Before we allow this union to lie, we shall
unveil the truth, aiming to create a lesson
to teach.

This engraved love is more than an "X"
and "O".
More than a game of "Tic TAC Toe"!
It's engraved deep; deeper than the
ocean.
It's also very steep, causing us to avoid a
certain motion.

In your arms of love I sleep, while being treated to a massage with your finest lotion.

This engraved love makes me weak.

Even though, it has strengths once I'm healed with your love potion.

So I engrave some more as we creep.

I must admit the second year feels just as sweet.

I savour the feel of this engraved love!

Merry Christmas!

Although the weather is cold and your
spirits are down,
I'm blessed to have you around.
Your presence makes my soul merry
despite the pain it carries.
Finding a gift was difficult because this
love is issued daily.
You rev me up like a Harley, and make me
feel as healthy as barley.

I pray we spend many more years like
this.
I enjoy each year during our Christmas
bliss.
The simplest things in life are our
blessings.
You are my blessing!
And what better time than Christmas
could I choose to tell you this?
You've taught me the true meaning of
love and happiness.

Every day I count the reasons why I love
you more.
You've made me realise true love is worth
waiting for.
I know I'm very lucky to have you in my
life.
You're all the many special things that
make a perfect wife!

Merry Christmas!

Happy Birthday.....celebrate in style!

One tree can start a forest like you've grown me.
One smile can win a friend like you've shown me.
One touch can show love and care.
You make my life worth living my dear.
It's like you own me.

Happy Birthday to my magical wife on your magical day!
Continue to wave your wand.
Be happy and embrace the chariots of tomorrow.
You're my violets of today,
My well arranged bouquet.

My "Trini Queen", my Angel Forever!
I love you!
My champion, my warrior, my cheerleader,
my one and all!
As we celebrate in style, I'll pick up your
heart if ever it falls.

Looking back on moments like these make
life worth living.
Smiles are heart melting,
And happiness is the remedy to any
amount of sorrow.
With your love, pain becomes an easier pill
to swallow.
No matter what speed bumps lie ahead,
we will overcome.
Look at how far we've come!

Happy Birthday my love, be blessed!
I will do my best to continue to cover you
so that your beautiful smile may beam
with never ending pride and love.

Our third Anniversary

From the first sight of you, I felt loved.
Three years of marriage and I feel it
even more!
I'm glad for our experiences and look
forward to the remaining journey and
excitement.

Like Kiss cakes, Shandy, shadow beni and
coriander, you've brought a unique flavour
to my life!
It's a flavour I don't want to fade away.
I can't imagine living another day
without you.
You've become my lover, friend, family and
my everything!

You are the sunshine on my face,
The blessing and grace.
The song that lifts my heart,
The joy that brightens all my days,
Right from the very start!

You are everything that makes my world
feel very special and brand new.
So thank you for how good it feels to love
someone like you!

Happy Anniversary
Three years down, forever to go!

Lovely Anniversary

My love,
Like a fruit tree, our hearts were very productive.
We accepted our destiny, nothing can stop this!
We were lost and free before our souls were made seductive.
You were very appealing to me, from day one, I loved this!

You mean more than the world to me.
We have faced countless challenges and claimed our victory.
We're not mad scientists but our creation blossomed through history.
We have experimented with our balances and unlocked a lovely mystery.

Our God is multi-talented for the way he made you for me.
Now the new challenge is, to enjoy this hickory flavoured anniversary!

Our flavour tastes very good, so we
repeat it times three!
It isn't smoked to perfection as yet and
could be better.
My love, I'm grateful for your affection
even when we're not together.
It's helping with our collection of love
that's worth more than any treasure!

The hands of time have rolled.
And through the years we've learnt to
allow our love to unfold.
Now we say cheers in a country that's
very cold.

Happy Anniversary!

Happy Valentine's Day!

It's a day for remembering our entire
happy yesterdays,
And looking forward to our wonderful
tomorrows.
I'm grateful for the joys and the sorrows.
It's a day for saying thank you,
Because nobody else could make me feel
the way you do!

You are still the amazing woman I fell in
love with.
And there is absolutely no one else who I
could imagine loving forever and ever.
You are and always will be the only one for
me, my Angel Forever!

Happy Valentine's Day
We will have many more to celebrate!

On your Birthday.....and always!

It's hard to remember the times when I didn't wake up with you beside me.
I can still feel the lovely nudges of your knee.
The longer we are together, the more I know that the best thing in my life is the love we share.
It's an absolute grace to know how much you care.
I always look forward to every moment with you my dear.

Thanks to you, we have memories that make me smile as much now, as the day we made them.
Reflecting always helps me to relive those beautiful moments, just as they were back then.

We've met challenges that I couldn't face
alone and no matter what life may bring I
have joy knowing you're on my side.
The longer we are together, the stronger
our love becomes.

This seems like the perfect time to tell
you that, the sweetest thing in my life is
the love we have created together!
A love I could only know with you.

Wishing you every ounce of happiness on
your birthday!

Our fourth Anniversary

I love you with all my heart.
To me, love is knowing absolutely
everything about someone and still
wanting to be with them more than
anyone else in the world.
I'm grateful to continue to have you as
my one and only girl.

On our special day, for me it's about
thanking my lucky stars that I found
someone as wonderful as you!

I'm grateful for the memories we are
creating as we dine tonight.
I will never forget our menu choices or
the tones of your face as the candles
burnt bright.

It's amazing how our love has aged like
fine wine.
Our unique flavour has become sweeter
with time.

Four blessed years is worth the world to me.
I'm forever grateful, as I bend on my knee.

        Happy Anniversary!

Quadruplets

The growth of quadruplets is risky.
Like a game of poker, we took a chance.
To conceive this much at once,
Doesn't require you to be extra frisky.
However, you will have to maintain the
romance.
To go through the birth requires
strength like whiskey.
We continue to be each other's support as
we lock hands.
Most people pray for this process to pass
by briskly.
However we are savouring each second of
our dance.

Now that we are here, we become four
times bigger;
Four times stronger;
Four times wiser!
We know this is just the appetiser.
The main course, we are left to figure.

We will not fall victim to hunger.
Throughout our journey we are our own
analyser.

Like any quadruplet, we must continue to
nurture it.
My love, enjoy the journey as we continue
to grow.
With number three in the rear view, we
have an opportunity to further it.
We will continue to love and benefit from
what we sow!
It doesn't matter if the world hasn't
heard of it.
The product of our union will always show!

Happy Anniversary
Four years down, forever to go!

Merry Christmas.....forever bright!

Just like the glow of candles on a peaceful night,
My love for you will shine forever bright!
You glow brighter than any ornaments graced by my sight.
While snow falls, you provide a source of light.

This holiday is always right on cue.
It reminds us of our love and the beginning of forever.
Even as the time flew, you remain my treasure.
The love we have together is wonderful and true.
I count myself so lucky to share my life with you.

You make everyday jolly.
You are as sweet as cake.
Your sugar can be moulded into a lolly.
I'm blessed to receive the carols our souls
make.

If I counted all the dreams that you
have made come true,
Then you would know the reason why I
love you the way I do!

Merry Christmas!

Happy Valentine's Day.....with all my love!

I thank my lucky stars I've got a
wonderful wife like you.
Just having you in my life has made my
dreams come true.

I know your feet must be tired because
you run through my mind daily.
This unique feeling is featured on the
front page of my old Bailey.
Our love during this valentine's season is
as unique as the sounds from a ukulele!

You're like a migraine because you are
constantly doing my head in.
And like Advil, it's upon your strength I
depend.

On a day like today, I'm not afraid to lay
roses at your feet.
Thank you my dear for giving me an
opportunity to speak.

You can take the keys to my heart and
bury it deeper than deep.
If I shall rise again, I want to rise for
only you!
Today, I pause to acknowledge my love
for you.

If you ever develop any doubt, take a look
in my eyes and they shall reveal my love is
true!
The true definition of love is how I feel
for you!

My message is quite simple.
I love you more than words can say.
And with you by my side, its Valentine's
every day!

You are the heart of my world and I love
you so very much!

Happy Valentine's Day!

You're my world

To my stunning wife,
I love you to the moon and back!
So far our journey is on track.
Each day with you is a blessed day.
I'm forever grateful, so each night I will
continue to pray!
You're wonderfully and fearfully made.
Your beautiful melanin can't be thrown any
shade!
I'm honoured to witness this day.
Your fourth birthday as my wife,
That's a very long time!
As we dine,
Lift your glass and toast to life!
Our life's journey needs to be enjoyed to
the fullest.

CHAPTER FIVE

What is love?

Love is staring into your eyes as my heart
soaks in your beauty.
You my dear, are more adorable than a
cutie.
The way my knees buckle in your presence
is a bit spooky.
You took my strength and brought out my
sensitive side even though I'm not fruity.

Love is exploring with your hand in mine.
It's that feeling of cold shivers as you
touch my spine.
It's getting lost and finding our directions
together.
It's crossing a frenzied highway in the
dessert with limited water.
It's jumping out of sleep to check on each
other.

Love is countless photos and unashamed
affection.
Love is creating memories and forgetting
them for new ones.

Love is protection.
It's reading boring poetry while providing
corrections.
Love is action.
Through the horrors of this world, you
provide a much needed distraction.

Love is trusting enough to share
everything about you, even the little
things you're embarrassed about.
It's being comfortable and relaxed
together but still getting those
butterflies when you catch each other's
eye.
Love is listening to snores and illegal foot
creaming.
Love is facing the uncertain and
supporting each other like rods to a
curtain.

It's missing each other when you're
apart and smiling at the thought of
shared moments and happy memories.
It's worrying about you and wanting you
to be safe.
It's the phone call or text that lets you
know I'm thinking of you.
It's hoping you will have everything that
will make you happy.
It's sharing in spirit and truth; mentally
and spiritually.
Love is enjoying each other's company.

Love can't be bought,
Your love is priceless.
You make my soul sing and my heart
ramble.
Your love fills and sustains me.
I've fallen in love with your soul and your
heart of gold!

My love

You're all my heart beats for.
Like guns to war, you've become a part of
my mere existence!
Look how far we've come.
I guess I'm rewarded for my persistence!
You stayed when you saw the slum,
And always kept me happy despite the
distance.

Like sand to the beach and waves to the
ocean, we caved in to become one.
Having each other's back was consistent.
You showed me true stardom.
For you my love, my heart has no
resistance.
I love you but this love is so much that
you can only have some!

Your love

My dear,
You alone can tame my hunger.
The love we share is a fiery flame way
over yonder.
Just one taste makes me wonder.
How can I make this love grow deeper?

It's a flavour so unique.
It has no comparison.
It's more than your physique.
Although that is a hot one!
This rare and wild fruit is my treat.
My favourite under the sun!
One bite takes my heart to sleep.
Please don't wake me until it's all done!

CHAPTER SIX

Surprises

I want to be full of surprises, like a
mystery box.
I want to push your adrenaline and catch
your heart when it drops.

I love to feel your warm embrace and your
heavy breathing in my ear.
That amazed look on your face lets me
know that I'm near.

I want to keep you guessing; wondering
what's next.
Will it be harmless caressing or will I
scare you to death?

I love to keep you in suspense, while my
actions increase your curiosity.
Things become intense and this gives me
the upper hand for more velocity.

I'll have many more disguises, when some
of the tactics flop.
Even if it's a bit feminine, your desires
remain on top.

There will be no shame or disgrace.
So you better beware of the strange
things in this place.
I'm just letting you know, to be fair.

To see you shocked is exciting,
 A job well done, I bet!
There will be no time for resting.
At least, not just yet!

The weather is too dense but that's a bit
of hypocrisy.
It adds a whole other sense to the way
we configure this remarkable mockery.
It takes time to realise this, like the
twisting of locks.
But some things I'll be better at like
removing accessories, even your socks!

Ecstasy

My love,

This union keeps me dreaming.

My soul is floating above the clouds.

We give love a whole new meaning.

I'm more than honoured to be your husband.

In your garden of roses, my spirits drift while I'm cleaning.

Your love enlightens my day, especially when your smile is beaming.

We will never go astray even if our pillars start leaning.

We have a bond that's unbreakable!

It doesn't matter who is scheming.

I just thought I'd let you know that you're forever "Queening".

To your arms of love my soul is clinging.

You always make me feel more than an ordinary human being!

These emotions can't be fathomed in any
amount of words.
We've blossomed deeper than just love
birds.
You're my soul mate, my Angel Forever!
Even amidst the strongest earthquake,
we'll prevail together!
So I'll pause in a moment of silence while
I soak in the harmony of your voice.
It's beautiful like melodies from violins.
That symphony is perfectly unforgettable!

Dilemma

You're not a bug, but certainly caught in a web!
How could you fly, if your wings aren't spread?
You spend the daytime dreaming,
Wishing upon the stars,
Forever trying to crack these mental bars!
Your movements are carried out carefully
so you don't receive any scars.

Your body lives in the eastern hemisphere,
Working to secure your life financially.
Your spirits traverse the western hemisphere,
Where you believe you will reside finally.
But cautious you are, you won't move blindly.
This burden has not fallen kindly.
You pray "Please God, may you guide me".
You're dreaming of sunshine, while you face these winters you dread.

You must admit, you are scared,
Especially with thoughts of living life
without the luxury of bread.
You try to trust in your other half,
But his lack of stability and assurance
doesn't suit your craft.
Oh my, you believe life has a grudge
against your laugh.

Should you trust God more?
Leap by faith?
You're missing the sandy seashore.
This is your life at stake.
You're used to an authentic core.
Your lifestyle can't tolerate anything
that's fake.
Those knock-offs will be rejected by your
store.
You reminisce on beautiful memories, while
enjoying a slice of red velvet cake.
What a dilemma!

You don't know what to do.
You pray "Father, I wish I was stronger
to have more faith in you".
This is your dilemma and it's very true.
Who ever knew, too many options could
bring sadness too!

To be continued!

AUTHOR'S MESSAGE

My love, this book of love is a small token to you on our 5th Wedding Anniversary. It highlights some of our high points, low points and the kinks in between. With love, many things are healed. I believe love gives us faith when things are tough. This will be an example for generations to come. It's one to be reflected upon and quoted like scriptures. I pray we never lose the ability to love. Long through our years to come, may love cover us so we may continue to shed light to the world!

I love you more!
Love Charmer

ACKNOWLEDGEMENTS

To my readers:

This book is dedicated to my wife. She is my backbone and my rib. We live in a cold world but knowing love like this still exists, brings a level of comfort to my soul.

To my wife:

I want to thank you my dear for embracing me and our destiny. Moreover, I thank you for your love! I pray that we are blessed with many more years to come. This book is just a small addition to our memorabilia. When you feel flustered or unsure about life, feel free to look back in here.

Thank you all!

Love Charmer

Printed in Great Britain
by Amazon

83043395R00061